Christi

The Great Battle

Living by Faith

by
Dwight Longenecker

*All booklets are published thanks to the
generous support of the members of the
Catholic Truth Society*

CATHOLIC TRUTH SOCIETY
PUBLISHERS TO THE HOLY SEE

Contents

1. Soldiers of Christ

Time and again a favourite story of mine has been voted the best book of the twentieth century. That book is Tolkien's *Lord of the Rings.*

 Not everybody is a fan of fantasy stories, and the adventures of a furry footed hobbit named Frodo simply doesn't interest some people at all.

However, the huge success of Tolkien's books and the blockbuster success of Peter Jackson's films indicate that there is something in the stories that keep people coming back for more.

At the very heart of The *Lord of the Rings* and every other classic tale, is the battle of good against evil. For a story to hold our attention there has to be conflict of some kind.

You may not be a fan of *Lord of the Rings* but whatever kind of story or film you like, conflict lies at the heart of the story. The villain may not be supremely evil. Indeed, the thing to be overcome might be the hero's circumstances, disability or personal problem. But whatever it is, there is some evil to be conquered if the hero is going to survive and thrive.

We are captivated by great stories in which the hero fights against evil because deep down we are all aware of some evil in our lives. Evil threatens us from the world around us, but it also threatens us from within. We have a deep instinct that unless we are involved in the battle against that evil we will quickly be swallowed up by it.

There must be good and evil

Some people think there is no such thing as good and evil. They say the world is simply neutral, and what seems good for you is what makes you feel good or helps you survive, while what seems bad is what you dislike, or what threatens you. So, for example, a deer will find a lion evil, but a lion will find a deer good.

This might be true for animals, but we are not animals. As human beings we have a higher understanding of free will and choice. In fact, at the very heart of our ability to choose anything at all, is the assumption that there is such a thing as good and evil.

Think about it for a moment. If I can choose between an apple and a chocolate bar, then I am assuming that one is better than the other. I may choose the chocolate bar even though I realise the apple would be better for me. If I do, I have convinced myself that the chocolate was a better thing for me after all, or that I will choose the apple next time. Choices are difficult, and deciding between good and evil is often tricky, but underlying even the most difficult choice is the assumption that good and evil exist - otherwise why do we agonise so much over the decision?

The very nature of choice demands the existence of good and evil because as soon as you choose you are making the assumption that the thing you chose is better than the thing you have rejected. You are therefore affirming the reality of good and evil.

It is true that making moral choices is more complicated than choosing between apples and chocolate bars, but the principle is the same. We choose to do certain things because we think they are good. We might be mistaken. What we thought was good may actually be bad for us, but even if we choose badly, at the heart of human choice is the reality of good and evil.

Common sense and the existence of evil

Some will still argue that what we call 'good' is simply what seems good for us and what we call 'evil' is what we think not good for us. They say that to live together peacefully we need to agree on some basic rights and wrongs. Good and evil are therefore just useful terms that help to oil the wheels of society. Can this be so?

It is strange that anyone could hold an opinion like this at the beginning of the twenty-first century. After all, in the last century we have experienced the most unimaginable evil the world has ever seen. More people have been mindlessly imprisoned, tortured, gassed and mutilated than ever before. Can we face the horrors of Auschwitz, the Rwanda massacres or the 'September 11th' attacks and shrug our shoulders and say, 'These things only seemed evil to the people who died that day'?

This simply won't do. If we have any morsel of humanity within us, then we must conclude that these, and many other examples, are examples of real, total and utter evil. Furthermore, one of the reasons this evil has grown is because the people who did it didn't think it was evil. The Nazis thought the elimination of the Jews was just a necessary act of ethnic cleansing. It is therefore the denial of the reality of good and evil that allows the most terrible evil to flourish.

To be honest, we have to admit that this evil is at work in the world right now. Furthermore, if we are really honest we will admit that there is a shadow side in all of us that would lead each one of us to commit horrific crimes if the circumstances were right.

We tell ourselves that we would not take part in mass murder, torture of innocent people or the rape and mutilation of defenceless children. But in the context of war and hardship we see that very ordinary people do, in fact, commit very horrific crimes - crimes of which they never thought they would be capable.

We cannot be neutral

The capability of terrible evil is present in every human heart, and it only takes the right circumstances to bring that beast within us to the surface.

You might agree that such a terrible beast does lurk in the shadow places of each human heart. You might also imagine that the beast is safely chained up in your dark places and that you would never do anything terribly wrong. That is what I would like to believe.

But I'm not so sure my dark side is totally under control. Are you sure yours is under control? When I lose my temper, when I give into selfish lust or greed and indulge myself, that beast soon starts showing his teeth. I start to become less patient and more violent towards those I live with. Furthermore, my own selfishness not only causes me to do bad things, it also keeps me from doing good things. The things I want to do I cannot and the things I do not want to do I do.

The fact of the matter is, each one of us is locked into this battle of good and evil every day of our lives. Furthermore, we are in the battle whether we like it or not. Because our human nature is selfish we are in conflict with other people whose natures are also selfish. Conflict lies at the heart of our daily existence.

We might wish to opt out of the conflict, but that is impossible too. If there really is a terrible evil out there, then, if we are good we must fight against it. There are only two choices: fight against the evil or give in to the evil. You cannot be neutral because being neutral is just another way of giving in to evil.

Usually the battle is clear

It is easy to make this battle more complicated than it actually is. We can imagine that the battle is difficult to understand. We can say that 'things are never so black and white' or 'it is never clear what is right and wrong.'

Some moral choices are difficult, but most are not. Most of the time moral choices are very easy. Living by those choices may not be easy, but the choice itself is easy. In most situations most people know what is right and what is wrong.

Religion gives us rules to live by, but society does too. The basic rules are universal to all human beings. The details might vary from one society to another, but the essential guidelines can be put quite simply: it is good to live for others and selfish to live only for ourselves. Being untruthful is wrong, telling the truth is right. Hurting others is wrong. Helping others is right. Stealing is wrong. Giving is right. Betraying loved ones is wrong. Being loyal is right.

In most situations, therefore, choosing what is right is easy. We may not have the courage and confidence to actually *do* what is right, but that is a different matter. If we can see what is right and wrong, then it is up to us to try our best to do the right thing and so help in the battle against evil.

You can make a difference

We would like to imagine that our own lives don't really matter when it comes to the great battle. We wish to be left on our own. We want to mind our own business. We don't think our own little lives are particularly selfish and we don't see why we should involve ourselves in the greater battle.

When faced with this complacency in my own life I try to turn around and ask myself why I should be exempt from the battle. Can I really stand by and do nothing? If there is a great battle between good and evil can I just hope for a quiet life and hope to avoid the conflict? What sort of a life is that? If I do not join in the battle, then I have wasted my life in easy comfort.

Instead of doing nothing, I should be using the life that has been given to me to make the world a better place. Each one of us wants life to have a purpose and meaning. The greatest purpose is the fight against evil. To sit around and do nothing in this battle is to condemn ourselves to a life that is empty and pointless.

Instead we can use our lives to enter the battle. Do we want to change the world? We must begin by changing ourselves. Do we think we are too small to make a difference? The world has always been changed by individuals, not by committees. There is a great and eternal destiny for each one of us if we will only join the battle. As one of the characters in the *Lord of the Rings* says, 'even the smallest person can change the world!'

You do not fight alone

The encouraging thing is that we do not fight alone in this battle. Every other human being is also engaged in the fight. In the midst of our ordinary, mundane lives we may not see the reality of this, but it is true: every person you meet is part of the monumental, cosmic battle against good and evil. Each person is fighting the shadows or giving in to the shadows a little bit more every day.

Because of this truth, you and I do not fight alone. Terrible situations in war and extreme social conditions show that the vast majority of human beings actually want to fight on the right side. No matter what their religion or belief system, most people understand the basic decent thing to do. Most people want to stand up for goodness and justice when they have the chance.

As a result, when you decide to enter the battle actively you will find that you are fighting alongside a whole host of other people. Human beings from every nation, from every religion and from every class of life will be there on your side fighting for honesty, peace, prosperity and goodness.

They do not only fight in the realm of ideas and great projects. The real battle goes on in the nitty gritty of everyday life. Those who are engaged in the battle know that the front line is in the home, the workplace, the schools and the community where they live. The war is huge, but every soldier who fights contributes his own humble and mundane part to the greater battle.

Christians believe that joining in this fight against evil is at the very heart of their own religious commitment. When a person is baptised they not only affirm their belief that Jesus Christ is the Son of God, and that he died for them. They do not then sit back and coast along to heaven when they die. Instead the Christian commitment is a commitment to take up arms in the great cosmic battle against evil.

Christians commit themselves to the battle for life. As they do, they join an army of others within their own community, around the world and down the ages who have also seen where the battle lines are and joined in to fight the good fight against the powers of darkness and the culture of death.

2. The Armies of
Darkness and Light

News reports, magazines and papers focus on the physical aspect of this battle. Every day when we hear the news or open a newspaper we are confronted with the reality of the fight between good and evil. The fight is there in almost every report if you have eyes to see it.

If a person has been raped or murdered, then the story is about the fight to capture the criminal and help the victims. If the news is about money and international finance, then the story is about poverty and wealth. If the news tells us about politics or peace negotiations, then the story is about power, peace and justice. Wherever you look, therefore, the battle between good and evil is a present reality.

The battle has a physical and historical dimension, but the battle is going on at a deeper level at the same time. The underlying battle is against the forces of darkness and destruction, and the forces of goodness and light. At this level the struggle is spiritual and moral - not just physical and historical.

Because we human beings are physical/spiritual beings it is possible for us to join in the battle in two different ways. We can fight on the side of goodness and light through our physical actions by doing good in the world, but we can also join in the spiritual battle against the forces of evil.

Christianity is a practical religion. It works. It helps us to fight the battle against evil on both levels at the same time. An active Christian does not simply pray about the troubles in the world and then do nothing. Neither does he simply work hard to make the world a better place. Instead the active Christian prays hard and works hard. He uses both physical weapons and spiritual weapons in the battle against evil.

The enemy is real

This is not just fantasy language or a symbolic way of looking at the world. The battle is real. Evil is real. Furthermore, that evil is planned and accomplished by real personalities. This is true on both the physical and spiritual levels.

When we consider the crimes committed by Hitler, Stalin or Osama bin Laden we can see that there are human beings who are genuinely given to evil. When we consider the crimes of a serial rapist or a sadistic child killer we realise that some people have given themselves to evil (even if they thought they were doing good). These human beings are the physical perpetrators of evil.

There are spiritual agents of evil as well. Down through ages, in every society there is evidence of malignant forces - real evil personalities who are purely spiritual and purely evil. Christians believe there are creatures who exist on a purely spiritual level. The good ones are called angels and the ones who have fallen into evil are called demons.

These evil spirits infest the world. They tempt people to commit crimes. If invited in, they can take over people's personalities and commit terrible atrocities through them. There is plenty of evidence from all over the world to show that these evil spirits really do exist and can influence individual lives and world events.

As a result, when we enter the battle against evil we will be opposed by evil human beings, but we will also be opposed by evil spiritual forces. We fight against the two different forces with different weapons. We use physical means to fight the physical battle, but we must use spiritual means to fight on the spiritual level.

Secret allies

Sometimes it might look like the forces of evil are winning, but those who fight within the Christian Church are fighting on the side that has already won. When Jesus Christ rose from the dead, death and evil were defeated. The war has not yet been completed, but the seed of evil's defeat has been planted, and the powers of darkness cannot win in the end.

When Jesus Christ founded the church he said 'the gates of hell will never be able to prevail against it.' In other words, those who follow Christ may lose some battles, but they cannot lose the war. As a result, when we become Christians and join the church we join a company of triumphant warriors.

The Christian has three types of secret allies that the forces of darkness have not reckoned with. First of all, when a person becomes a Christian he immediately has a whole range of allies all across the world. All those who also follow Christ have become his brothers and sisters. They have become his fellow foot soldiers. Like him, they are committed to the battle and fight by his side.

A Christian is also joined by the vast multitude of fellow Christians who have left this physical life, but still live in the spiritual realm. All those who have died in the faith of Christ still live in his victory.

They are still interested and involved in the battles going on here on planet earth. When Christians love and pray to the saints, they are enlisting their help and prayers for the ongoing battle.

Those who fight for the right also have the help of the spiritual powers who are on the side of goodness and light. Angels are God's messengers. They are also our helpers. In the spiritual battle they are committed to strengthening, guiding and protecting us in the battle. We do not fight alone. The angels and our fellow Christians - both alive and dead in Christ - fight by our side.

Secret weapon

As human beings we have a unique secret weapon in this battle. We have our bodies. The angels and demons are purely spiritual beings. In this physical world they are therefore disadvantaged. The animals are purely physical beings and cannot consciously join in the fight. But we are a special and amazing blend of spiritual and physical. As a result we can fight on both the physical and spiritual level at the same time: something the angels and demons cannot do.

When you think about it, this is a most amazing quality. We fight evil by fasting, praying and worshipping God. But we can also fight evil by making an apple pie and walking across the street to deliver it to Mr Franklin - that depressed and housebound neighbour.

Because we are a blend of physical and spiritual the best weapons in the battle are always both physical and spiritual at the same time. Taking an apple pie to Mr Franklin is one thing, but praying for Mr Franklin and helping him to find strength in the midst of his darkness through prayer and meditation is even better.

Because we are physical/spiritual beings we can fight the battles against evil in a unique and powerful way. This is our strength, but it is also our downfall. If we can fight evil with both body and spirit, then we can also be defeated through the wrong use of both body and spirit. In us human beings, the spiritual and the physical are linked both for good and for evil.

Physical weapons
Our bodies are our physical weapons in the battle. The New Testament says our bodies 'are the temple of the Holy Spirit'. In other words, our bodies are the dwelling place of the Holy Spirit, and it is through our bodies that the Holy Spirit of Christ can conduct his battles against evil.

Our hands therefore become the hands of Christ in the world. Our lips speak his words and our feet can run to do his will. With our bodies we live and move in the physical realm and with our bodies we fight in the battle. When we help the sick, feed the hungry or visit the prisoners we are using our bodies to fight evil.

Our bodies are not simply shells for our souls. Our soul does not inhabit a body as a person sits inside a car. Instead our bodies and souls are united in a single being. Our souls reside in our bodies more as water in a sponge than water in a cup. Because of this, our spiritual health and our physical health are interlinked.

What we do with our bodies, therefore, can affect the state of our souls, and likewise, what we do with our souls can affect the state of our bodies. It will be difficult to pray and worship, for instance, if our bodies are addicted to the poison of drugs and alcohol. It will also be impossible to pray and worship if our minds are full of hatred and vengeful thoughts, envy, pornographic images, greedy ambitions, fear and pride.

Likewise, what we do with our souls impacts on our bodies and minds. If we pray, if we submit to God's way, if we ask for the Holy Spirit to fill our lives and guide us, then we will benefit physically and mentally. Many studies have shown that religious people are generally happier, live longer, are more prosperous and more well adjusted. People who pray and meditate enjoy better health, have better marriages, live longer, heal faster and are more optimistic about the future.

Spiritual weapons

The physical weapon in the battle may be our bodies, but the spiritual weapons are our mind and soul. Prayer and worship is like exercise for the soul. It is also the way the soul engages in the spiritual battle against evil.

It is easy to forget that there is a spiritual dimension to the battle against evil. It is also easy to imagine that we can do nothing worthwhile in the spiritual realm. This is not so. We can have great spiritual power, and learn how to use that power for good.

The way to develop that spiritual power is to ask to be filled with the Holy Spirit. The Holy Spirit enables us to understand the rules of battle. The Spirit helps us discern the best way to fight, and where to focus our energy. The Holy Spirit also gives us the spiritual energy to take up the fight.

We stay tuned in to the Holy Spirit through prayer, meditation, contemplation and worship. Prayer is focussed spiritual energy. Prayer is a way to align our will with God's will in order to accomplish great things in the spiritual realm. I will say more about prayer later, but it is enough at this point to say that there are many different forms of prayer, and each person needs to find what works best for them. Through prayer and worship we work with God to fight against evil in the spiritual realm, but just fighting in one of the two realms isn't good enough.

3. The Most Powerful
Weapons of All

Because we are both spiritual and physical creatures we fight the battle against evil in both spiritual and physical ways. Physical actions against evil are the good deeds that we do. Spiritual actions are prayer, meditation and worship.

But it is artificial to separate the spiritual from the physical. Within us the spiritual and physical dimensions are totally one. Our physical actions have spiritual meaning and our prayers involve our bodies. One of the results of God taking human form in Jesus Christ is that the barrier between the spiritual and physical realms was broken forever.

In Jesus the spiritual and the physical are perfectly united. If we are to become more like Jesus, then we should be moving closer to that same unity between the physical and spiritual realms.

Part of the battle against evil is this very battle. Those who are given to evil are deeply divided within, and their spiritual and physical natures are at war. Those who are moving towards goodness are also moving towards wholeness and inner unity. When we pursue the good we are also working to unify our spiritual and physical dimensions.

To bring us into this unity Christians have been given special weapons for the battle that combine the spiritual and the physical in one action. These weapons are called 'sacraments'. The word 'sacrament' means 'mystery' but it also means 'covenant'. A covenant is a solemn promise between two parties that is sealed by a physical action. So, for example, a marriage covenant is sealed with rings or a peace treaty might be sealed with a ceremony in which swords are exchanged then solemnly broken.

In a sacrament we participate in a solemn ceremony which is physical and spiritual at the same time. The physical aspect of the sacrament actually seals and effects what it symbolises spiritually. For example, when two people make love that physical action seals their marriage and a physical-spiritual bond is actually established between them.

The same is true of all the sacraments. They are formal, solemn ceremonies in which a physical action affects and transforms our spiritual condition. As a result, sacraments are extremely powerful weapons in the ongoing battle against evil.

There are many physical actions and objects that can carry spiritual meaning and affect our spiritual condition. Candles and icons, holy buildings and sacred sites, beautiful music, architecture and paintings can all have a wonderful spiritual effect and strengthen us spiritually. The beauties of nature, the love of our families and the simple physical joys of life can all help us spiritually and strengthen us in the battle. But there are seven particular things that Christians recognise as having a formal sacramental effect in our life.

Joining and belonging

On the Day of Pentecost Jesus' followers received the gift of the Holy Spirit. Peter was their appointed leader, and when he stood up to speak he explained to the crowd that to follow Christ they need to turn away from their selfish ways, believe in Christ and be baptised.

Baptism is the first sacrament of the Christian life. When a person is baptised there is a spiritual dimension: faith, and a physical dimension: being put into water. Being plunged into water symbolises cleansing, but it also symbolises re-birth. In addition, it represents the fact that by believing in Christ we are plunged into his death and resurrection.

If we are baptised as an adult then we make our own declaration of belief in Christ. This is called a 'profession of faith.' When a baby is baptised the profession of faith is made on their behalf by their parents and sponsors (godparents).

As the person is plunged into the water or has water poured over him, the person who is baptising proclaims that this solemn action is done in the name of the Father, the Son and the Holy Spirit. This is to show that through baptism we enter into the very life of God himself, and God's life enters into us.

The sacrament of baptism cleanses us from that inborn tendency to do wrong called original sin. It also gives us the power to live God's way and decide to follow his will in our lives. At that point the Holy Spirit begins to work in our lives to enable us to take part in the great battle against evil, sin and death.

The sacrament of confirmation is when a baptised person is formally received into the Church. After a suitable time of instruction the baptised person decides that he or she wants to be a full member of the Church. At that point a church leader (usually the bishop) lays his hands on the person's head and anoints them with blessed oil. This formal blessing symbolises the father's blessing of his child, and through this physical-spiritual action a person is made a full member of the Church family.

In a way, what was begun at baptism is completed at confirmation. At that point the person makes sure or 'confirms' his earlier decision, or the decision that was made for him by his parents if he was baptised as an infant.

Keeping on line

At baptism God cleanses us from original sin and gives us the power to fight the good fight of faith. But in that war we often lose some battles. It is not easy to follow Christ, and we fight against powerful enemies. The spiritual forces of darkness will do their best to make us fall into selfishness, sin, violence and evil.

We also have to fight against our own fallen nature. Baptism gives us the power to fight, but it doesn't mean we are made perfect overnight. Our own effort, co-operating with the power of the Holy Spirit, is required if we are to win the battle.

When we fail, members of our team pick us up and help us keep going. Remember, we are fighting as part of a great army, and it is part of an army's duty to set up ambulances, rescue teams and field hospitals to help those who have fallen in battle.

When we fall back into the darkness of selfishness, lust, anger and violence we have a way back into a good relationship with God. Forgiveness is God's way of putting us back into the same clean and whole condition we first received at our baptism.

We receive that forgiveness through the sacrament of reconciliation or confession. Confession is a powerful weapon in the battle against evil. At that point we speak to a priest. We simply tell him what we have done wrong and ask him to pray with us for God's forgiveness.

Jesus gave his disciples the power to forgive sins on earth just as he had done, and that power continues to be present and available to us through the ministry of the priest in the sacrament of reconciliation. Through that gift we get a fresh start, the power to change and continue our fight against evil.

Forgiveness and healing

When Jesus was on earth his power to forgive was always linked with his power to heal. Since the

Church is the body of Christ on earth, the church still has the power to do what Christ did. The Church is our army in the battle. It is there to help us be equipped for the battle, to fight well and to be healed when we have been wounded.

Healing is administered in the church in various ways. Some people in the church have a counselling ministry. These people help us to find inner healing. Others have the ministry of spiritual direction. They help us to find spiritual healing and strength. Still others have the gift of physical healing. By laying hands on the sick they are sometimes healed physically.

There is also a formal sacrament of healing. In this sacrament the physical element is blessed oil. The spiritual element is turning from our own way and having faith in Christ's healing power. The formal sacrament of healing is usually reserved for cases of extreme illness, and many priests and people report that real, physical healings often take place when the sacrament is administered.

In other cases the person is healed in an inner way. They may find new relief from pain, greater peace of mind and a new strength to cope with their illness. Often the family members of the one who is anointed find new strength and spiritual help in their time of need.

When a person is anointed at the very end of their life it is called 'extreme unction' or 'the last rites'. Sometimes the sacrament actually brings the person back from death's door for a longer period of life. Most often the last rites prepare the person for a peaceful death and assure him or her that all shall be well, and they can depart in peace.

Forming a squadron

In every army there are subgroups - small, united, well bonded fighting units. This is not a bad way to think of a Christian family. God loves to work through the power of human love and family ties. When a man, woman and children are bound together in a deep and abiding love they provide a sleek, powerful fighting force against the forces of darkness.

The powers of darkness hate pure, solid and sensible family love. That is why the powers of darkness tempt us with sexual sin - because they do not want us to be part of a solid, pure and happy marriage. They do not want children born into the world if they are going to be born into a happy Christian family.

This is why Christians have always been devoted to building up the family. The sexual instincts are a powerful force. Through them love is expressed and comes to abundance in the lives of new children. Within a Christian marriage and family life there is great fruitfulness, great power for good and therefore a great potential for victory over evil.

Forming a Christian marriage, is therefore one of the best ways anyone can fight against the powers of evil in the world. To find a man or woman who is as devoted to the fight as you are, and then marrying them and building a strong Christian family is to win one of the most tremendous battles against the forces of darkness possible.

That is why the Church has said that marriage is a sacrament. In marriage the physical and the spiritual are joined in a marvellous and miraculous way. When a husband and wife make love they are sealing with a physical action a union that is spiritual and eternal.

That love is meant to produce children, and when the possibility of children is artificially eliminated from the action of making love that relationship of love is reduced to selfishness between the two people. This is a victory for the evil side because two people who were supposed to be living a radiant life of self-sacrifice and love, have chosen selfish pleasure instead. An action of love that was supposed to bring new life into the world has been used instead for mere personal pleasure.

Taking Orders

In the Christian battle there are some people who are professional soldiers. These are the ones who are uniquely dedicated to the battle. They have no other claims on their time. They are the specialists and the experts. They are available to go anywhere and serve God totally in the battle against evil.

When a man is ordained as a priest, or when a man or woman becomes a monk or a nun they are specially dedicated to serve God only. This is why they also take a vow of celibacy. The vow of celibacy doesn't mean they think sex is wrong. They believe sex is wonderful, but that it belongs to marriage and family life. Because they have decided to serve God alone, they have given up family life and therefore have given up sexual relationships.

The formal sacrament of ordination is reserved for those men who are called to be priests. Priests are present day representatives of the twelve apostles Jesus first called and dedicated to lead the church. The priesthood is reserved to men because, despite having many devout women disciples, Jesus did not choose any of them for the special task of being a priest.

The priesthood is reserved to men not because women are inferior, but because different roles are appropriate for men and women. The different roles are not only between men and women. In fact all Christians are called to be priests because all of us are called to fight the good fight of faith and minister God's love to the world. But we are not all *ordained* as priests because within the battle we exercise our priesthood in a multitude of different ways.

When a priest is ordained the bishop and other priests lay hands on his head and he is anointed with oil for his new role in life. This is the physical aspect of the sacrament. The spiritual element is the man's calling, dedication to service and faithful vow to serve Christ as a priest.

In each of these sacraments we are given a physical/spiritual weapon to help us in our physical/spiritual lives. The seven sacraments are God's way of helping us through every stage and decision point in our lives. From baptism as an infant through confirmation, marriage, reconciliation and final last rites; the Church like an army or like a faithful family, is there to help us in the journey and equip us for the battle at hand.

But you may have noticed that I spoke of seven sacraments and only discussed six. The seventh is the greatest and needs a separate section of its own.

4. The Ultimate Weapon

There is one physical-spiritual weapon that is the greatest of all. In the last week of his life, Jesus gathered his apostles together and celebrated a ceremonial meal with them.

When the Jewish people were enslaved in Egypt God told them to sacrifice a young lamb and put the blood on the doorposts and lintels of their houses. When the angel of death saw the blood he would pass over their homes and spare them. Every year after that the Jewish people celebrated the same 'Passover' meal. They killed a lamb, which they called 'the Lamb of God'. As they ate the ceremonial meal, they re-lived their salvation from death and their delivery from slavery.

Jesus' last meal with his apostles was this same Passover meal. At the meal they read the Old Testament story of the Passover then celebrated the meal once again. At the meal they not only ate the lamb that had been sacrificed, they also ate bread and drank wine. As they shared this ancient ceremonial meal Jesus added a new dimension to it.

Jesus took the bread, blessed it and broke it. He then said, 'This is my body which is given up for you.

Do this in remembrance of me.' Then he took the cup, blessed the wine and said, 'This is my blood of the new covenant. Drink this in remembrance of me.'

Remember the word 'covenant' means sacred promise or a solemn agreement between two parties. John the Baptist had called Jesus 'the Lamb of God', and there at the Passover supper Jesus said he was going to die for his friends. He was therefore the Lamb of God who would be killed to deliver them from death and slavery.

Jesus transformed the Jewish ceremonial meal into a new kind of meal. Now it was not to commemorate the ancient delivery from slavery and death, but the delivery from slavery and death that he was to accomplish. Jesus told his apostles to celebrate this physical/spiritual covenant or 'sacrament' until the end of time.

I am with you

Jesus also promised his apostles that he would be with them until the end of time. After he rose from the dead his apostles realised that he was with them in an astounding way through the ceremonial meal that he had commanded them to continue.

In a disturbing lesson, Jesus had told his followers that they could not have life within them unless they ate his flesh and drank his blood. Obviously he was not telling them to be cannibals, so what could he possibly have meant? It all came clear when he celebrated the Passover meal with them. When he said the bread was his flesh and the wine was his blood they remembered that he had said you cannot have spiritual life within you unless you eat his flesh and drink his blood.

This same ceremonial meal has been continued for the last two thousand years. In a multitude of ways all over the earth, every day this sacred meal is celebrated with reverence, devotion and care. Why do Christians take such care and spend so much time on this strange ceremony involving bread and wine?

It is because we really believe that Jesus Christ who died and rose again is with us through the bread and wine. We believe that the bread and wine have been transformed into his body and blood. We do not believe that if you took the bread and wine into a laboratory it would turn out to be human flesh and blood. Instead, we believe that its inner reality is transformed by God's power into Jesus' flesh and blood. One way to explain what we believe happens is to say that the bread's 'bread-ness' and the wine's 'wine-ness' have become the flesh and blood of Jesus Christ.

The sacraments are physical/spiritual realities. They are not just symbols. They are not just good ideas. We have bodies and souls blended together. Both are real. Therefore, God chooses to work in us through real bread and real wine that have really been transformed by Christ's action into his own body and blood.

Battle rations

Every army needs battle rations. Every pilgrim needs food for the journey. In the *Lord of the Rings* the travellers are given a special *lembas* bread that never gets stale and gives them supernatural strength. In the Old Testament exodus story the Jewish people were given *manna* - which was a special bread from heaven for their journey. When he was on earth Jesus fed a crowd by miraculously dividing a little boy's lunch.

The 'bread from heaven' was not only the *manna*. The Jewish people also considered their sacred writings to have come from God, and so they referred to their Scriptures as 'bread from heaven' as well. The bread in the Passover meal gives a spiritual-physical nourishment while the Scriptures nourish the mind and spirit.

When Jesus told his apostles to celebrate the memorial meal until the end of time he was commanding them to provide supernatural food for the troops. The successors of the apostles are the bishops and priests of the church. By a direct historical line every valid Catholic priest can trace the fact that by his ordination he is descended from the apostles. Because of this, he is the one who is authorised to preside at the celebration of this ceremonial meal which is called the Eucharist or the Mass.

The bread and wine do not become Christ's body and blood by the priest alone. Instead the risen Lord Jesus Christ performs the miracle through the priest. When he does so we receive our physical/spiritual food for the journey. When we eat the consecrated bread and drink the wine we receive Christ's body and blood in a real and powerful way. The elements enter our body and our bloodstream and we receive physical/spiritual strength.

Christ is with us in this way more powerfully and wonderfully than we ever could have imagined. This is not simply a religious symbol or a spiritual idea. It is a powerful reality. Many Christians will relate how the blessed bread and wine have helped them on the journey, and how going to the Eucharist meal every week has helped them make their way through life.

The power to change

It has been said that 'you will become like the thing you worship'. This assumes that all of us worship something, but often we are not aware of what we worship. The way to figure out what we worship is to ask ourselves what it is that we live for and what it is that we would be willing to die for. That is the thing we worship.

Do we worship our job? We might think that we are not willing to die for our boss, but if we devote the sort of lifestyle to our job that is slowly killing us, then maybe we are willing to die for our job after all. Do we worship the money that our job brings? Do we worship pleasure? If we are willing to risk our lives for that pleasure, (through overindulgence, risky sex or drugs) then we are willing to die for that thing.

Jesus Christ simply asks us to get our priorities right and to worship the only One who is worthy of our worship - and that is God. The word 'Eucharist' means 'thanksgiving', and when we go to the Eucharist we are worshipping God and giving thanks for all that he has done in our lives.

We do this by worshipping Jesus Christ who is God in human form. If you become like the thing you worship, then we choose to worship Jesus Christ because, as the God-Man, he is the one we want to be like. As we receive him into our lives by eating his body and drinking his blood at the Eucharist we really do receive the power to become like him.

This is what worship is all about, and by focussing on Christ at the Eucharist we immediately put all other false objects of worship into their rightful place. That's why we are expected to go to Mass every week - because we need a constant correction of our priorities. To fight well, we need to get focussed and get our bearings time and time again.

Getting focussed

When we attend Mass every week we are getting focussed on the reason why we are on this earth. We are not here for our own pleasure. We are not here to acquire as much money as possible. We are not here to simply float through life trying not to be bored. We are here for a purpose. We are here to join in the fight against the powers of darkness and evil.

We cannot do this unless we bind ourselves to Christ, who already won the victory against evil. We do this first in baptism and confirmation, but we renew our covenant with Christ through the sacrament of reconciliation, and by receiving communion regularly.

At Mass we hear several passages of the Bible being read. The priest speaks for a short time to give us advice in the physical/spiritual battle we are a part of. The Bible is God's word to us. When we hear the Bible at Mass we are receiving spiritual food for our mind and soul.

After that we celebrate the ceremonial meal together. Just as Christ did, the priest takes the bread, breaks it and blesses it. He then gives it to us as food for the journey, and as the living presence of Christ in our lives.

This meal is central to the lives of all committed Christians. Christianity is not about trying hard to be good. It is not about studying the teachings of Jesus to understand a spiritual way better. It is not about working hard to make the world a better place. It is first and foremost about staying in touch with Christ, and keeping his Spirit alive in our lives. Receiving him in this physical/spiritual way at Mass is the most vibrant, real and powerful way to stay in touch with Him.

Taking action

The sacraments are the physical/spiritual weapons for our battle against evil. They are at the heart of the Christian life, because no soldier can go into battle without training, equipment and rations.

The sacraments are vitally important, but they are not the whole story. The formally religious dimension is part of the picture, but the whole of life is bigger than that. The formal aspect of religion is a bit like an army training camp, the hierarchy of the officers and receiving the necessary provisions, instructions and equipment for battle.

The sacraments are like our weapons; they are not an end in themselves. They are given to help us live a new kind of life, not to be that life. In any battle the weapons are important, but they are not the actual battle. Winning the battle is what matters. The weapons are simply the means to that end.

The sacraments equip and strengthen us for the battle, but we actually engage in the Christian battle by living our lives day by day. Within our daily lives there are many ways to fight the battle. The battle is fought spiritually and physically, and I would now like to turn from the weapons to the battle itself.

5. Changing Yourself

Your spiritual life is like a mill. You put grain in and you get flour out. If you don't put something good in, then you can't get something good out. It's as simple as that. Our minds need to be filled with good things if our lives are going to produce a good product.

In our media saturated world it is difficult not to have our minds filled with lots of poisonous trash. Much of the content of popular music, television, films and magazines is simply harmless fun. It entertains and amuses us, and that's good. However, there is much in the media that fills our minds with rubbish. Sometimes the rubbish is simply boring trivia that occupies space on our mind's hard drive that should be used for better material. Other input from films, television, music and advertising is genuine trash that poisons our imagination, pollutes our minds and works as one of the agents of the dark side.

If we are fighting a spiritual battle, then we will make sure that we fill our minds with all that is good, true and beautiful. We should take time for the natural goodness of the world around us. We should open our minds to the best music, literature, art and culture. We should learn to enjoy all that builds us up and opens our minds to the best in other cultures.

One of the best ways to win this aspect of the battle is to take time to read good books. The mind is engaged with ideas in a fresh way when we discover good reading material in books, on the internet or through enlightening films and theatre.

For a Christian, one of the key sources of learning and enlightenment are the documents of the faith. The writings of the saints, the words of worship and the Bible all contribute to building up the mind and putting goodness in so goodness can come out.

The good book

The Bible is made up of two sections: the Old Testament and the New Testament. The Old Testament records the religious history of the Jewish people as well as their religious poetry, sermons and hymns. The New Testament begins with four versions of the story of Jesus Christ called the gospels. The rest of the New Testament is the story of the foundation of the Christian Church and letters of instruction that the apostles wrote to the first Christians.

Christians believe the Bible is inspired by God. It didn't just drop out of heaven. Neither was it dictated to the human writers by an angel or the Holy Spirit. Instead, the Holy Spirit inspired or 'breathed into' the writers in a more subtle way. The Holy Spirit infused the Biblical authors with the insights, ideas and the power to express them properly. We also believe that the same Holy Spirit uses the Bible today to inspire and enlighten us as we read it.

Pick up and read

Therefore, every Christian should have a Bible and read it. It is difficult, however, to decide how and when to read the Bible. Some people simply start at the beginning and read a chapter a day. But the most difficult parts of the Bible are at the beginning, and therefore most people get bogged down after a week or two.

The best way of reading the Bible is to read it with the whole church, day by day and week by week. When we go to Mass a section of the Old Testament, an ancient Jewish hymn called 'a psalm' and a section of the New Testament is read. Then a portion from one of the gospels is read. All these weekly portions are collected in a book called a Missal. If you have a missal you will have handy and accessible portions of the Bible to read day by day and week by week.

Other people use Bible reading notes. These are published in a little magazine that you can buy in Christian bookshops or order by post. It gives you a portion of the Bible to read every day and provides a few paragraphs to explain the Bible passage and apply it to your life.

It is possible to study the Bible in depth, or simply to read it to learn more about one's faith. But the Bible is best read in an atmosphere of prayer. You should ask the Holy Spirit to open your eyes to the truths in the Bible and to help you understand what you read and apply it in your life. The wisdom and the words of the Bible really do have a power to transform lives, and if you want to get energy and light for the battle against the darkness, then read the Bible and learn how to pray.

Keeping in touch

Prayer is absolutely vital for the spiritual life. No one can grow as a Christian unless they learn how to pray, and we learn how to pray as we learn how to swim or ride a bike - by doing it.

Many people's ideas of prayer are linked with a childhood understanding of prayer. They imagine that prayer consists of asking God for things they want. Certainly there is one dimension of prayer that consists of asking God for what we want, but prayer is much greater than that. Someone once well said, 'prayer doesn't change God, it changes me.'

In other words, we pray to align ourselves with God's will. When Jesus taught his disciples to pray he instructed them to say to God, 'May your will be done on earth as it is in heaven.' In other words, they were subjecting their own will to God's will. Through prayer they were trying to find out what God wanted - not tell him what they wanted. That's why, when a Christian asks God for anything he or she ends the request by saying, 'If it is your will.'

So real Christian prayer is asking God for the things that are his will. You might then ask, what is the point? If it is his will won't it happen anyway? But there is a mysterious action going on in prayer. When we pray we align our will with God's; but we sometimes forget that the human will is a very strong force. When we align our will with God's the two together become a powerful force for good. If you look at it this way, prayer is like surfing. God's will is the big wave coming in. I am trying to find out where its going, then to go with it and ride the wave. With the two forces together great things can be accomplished in the battle against evil.

Purifying the mind

Many religions teach their followers to meditate. Meditation is known to have marvellous beneficial effects. People who meditate regularly have less stress. They live longer. They are happier and they deal with problems in a more confident way. People who meditate enjoy better health, better relationships and a better quality of life.

In the Eastern religions the meditation technique is to empty the mind and simply dwell in the eternal silence. This activity slows down the mind waves and allows the person who is meditating to enter into a calmer, more peaceful state of being.

Christian meditation is different. Christians use the word 'meditation' for another kind of mental activity. When Christians meditate they take a story from the gospels or a word or phrase from the Bible and they 'bathe themselves' in that idea, phrase or mental image. They relax into the particular phrase or idea or image until it goes deep into them and they become part of it.

Many Christians use the rosary as a way of doing this. The rosary is a pattern of repetitious prayers. These prayers help to calm the mind and take the person to a deeper state of consciousness. At the same time, the person is expected to focus on a particular event in the life of Jesus. As they say the prayers and enter into this deeper state they also enter more deeply into the life, ministry, death and resurrection of Jesus. In this way their life is merged with his life and they become more like him.

This is a more positive and objective form of meditation than the Eastern religions practice. It doesn't just call for an empty mind, it is full of real and powerful content. Christian meditation is just as calming and peaceful as Eastern meditation, but it is also meaningful, and as such it is a simple and powerful way to get closer to Christ and engage in the spiritual battle against evil.

The still point of the turning world

The Christian practice that is most like the meditation of Eastern religions is what we call contemplation. In contemplative prayer a person is taken beyond meditation on a particular image, phrase or story.

When a person enters into contemplation they simply dwell in the presence of Christ.

This sounds rather strange. It isn't. Have you ever spent an evening with someone you love and realise that you don't have to talk or play a game or go out somewhere? It is fine simply to be together. Maybe you are reading while they are doing a puzzle or knitting. You don't need to talk to one another. You can simply 'be' together.

Contemplation is like that, except that the other person we are with is Jesus Christ. In the forms of meditation taught by the Eastern religions the person meditating is supposed to empty their mind, but in Christian contemplation we fill our mind with the presence of Christ.

An old peasant woman was asked how she prays. She said, 'I just sit and look at Him and he sits and looks at me.' That simple peasant was a real contemplative, and her words fit in with the experience of millions of Christians. The greatest saint of modern times, a young Frenchwoman named Thérèse Martin said that contemplation was to 'gaze on the face of Christ.'

This can be practised at home. If you have an icon of Christ or one of the saints, set it up and light a candle. Sit still and focus your gaze on the scene before you and clear you mind. Simply let go of all the thoughts that cram into your head. Imagine they are floating away like a helium filled balloon. Focus on the image before you until you are looking through the image to the presence beyond.

Another way to 'gaze on the face of Christ' is in the traditional service of Benediction or 'adoration of the Blessed Sacrament.' In this simple act of worship the consecrated bread from the Eucharist is displayed on the altar in a large receptacle called a monstrance. The simple white disc becomes the focus point for our contemplation of Christ, and through this action we enter into his presence in a way far beyond all words and description.

Communities of prayer

Prayer is so important to the spiritual struggle that there are communities of people who live together to devote their lives entirely to prayer. Monks and nuns give up all other ambitions to spend their whole lives in prayer.

This doesn't mean they spend every moment of every day on their knees in church. Instead they try to live out a life in which prayer is the heartbeat of every moment. Monks and nuns *do* spend much time in actual prayer, but they are also trying to bring prayer into every moment of life so that every action and thought also becomes totally given to God, and so becomes a kind of prayer.

There are a vast number of different communities of prayer all over the world. Some are for men only, some for women only. Some have married couples and families living together with celibate people. Some are totally enclosed and traditional. In these communities the men and women rarely go out and pursue a totally inner life of study and prayer.

Other communities are more modern and are engaged in activities to promote the Christian faith, work for justice and peace and to help the disadvantaged, disabled and poor. In these communities the devoted men and women combine prayer with action in a life of total dedication.

These special communities are part of the whole Church, but each local church or parish, is also supposed to be a community of prayer. As we meet together with one another and in our own homes, we are constantly fighting the battle against evil by learning how to pray.

Getting together

The local community gets together every week to do together what each Christian should have been doing on his own throughout the week. At Mass we pray, read the Bible, focus on Christ and re-commit ourselves to the battle we first signed up to in our baptism.

Christian worship has a basic structure called the liturgy. This structure is provided by the Church, and it is the same basic structure that has been used for the last two thousand years.

In this structure we do not use our own words to worship God, but the words that are shared by the whole of God's family. Using a set structure does two things. First it ensures that the words of worship are purely Christian, and that they have not been infected with false ideas. Second, it binds us together with all other Christians who have used and are using these same words.

While we use the same set structure, the actual worship may vary widely. The music and style of using these words can be very different depending on where you go. Therefore in one place the Mass may be a solemn High Mass with classical music and a fine choir. In another place the music will be provided by a group of local people playing instruments and singing simple hymns. If you go to Africa or South America the style will be very different indeed, but the basic structure and the content will be the same.

This unity in the midst of diversity is one of the great strengths of the Catholic Church. In it we can all worship the same Lord Jesus Christ. We can all commit to the same battle, and yet we can also be ourselves and worship God in a language and style that is right for us.

6. Changing the World

Prayer, worship and reading are not the end goal of the practice of the Christian religion. Like the sacraments they are only the means to an end. We do these things because by them our lives are transformed. By prayer, worship and the practice of religious sacraments God comes alive in our lives and we gradually grow into the radiant, strong and confident people we were created to be.

Becoming all we can be is part of the point of religious practice, but Christianity has never simply been about personal fulfilment or salvation. From the very beginning Christianity, like the Jewish faith from which it developed, has been a communal religion.

It is impossible to be a totally solitary Christian. To be a Christian means we belong to the body of Christ and that body is made up of all the other people in the world and down the ages who have also followed Christ. To be a Christian means belonging to the Christian family.

That means we are responsible for one another. We also recognise that all other people are also part of that family in a larger way. They may not believe in

Jesus Christ, but they are also our brothers and sisters inasmuch as they are part of the same human race.

Being a Christian means we are involved with all other people. We are called to be concerned about their welfare and to do as much as we can to help them. We do not ask God to change us through prayer, worship and personal renewal just for our own gratification. We ask him to change us so that we can go on to change the world.

Missionaries of charity

Mother Teresa of Calcutta is an excellent example of how prayer and action go together. Mother Teresa was a nun. Her life was devoted to prayer, meditation and contemplation. For many years she taught in a convent school for middle-class Indian girls. But through her prayer she also became aware that she should be serving the poorest of the poor in the slums of Calcutta. If Mother Teresa had only been interested in her own salvation she would not have had the eyes to see the suffering of others.

Prayer helped her to see what ought to be done. Eventually she founded a little community of women who were devoted both to prayer and to a ministry to the poorest of the poor. Mother Teresa and her nuns would start each day with an hour of meditation and then worship God at the Eucharist. Each working day was punctuated with times of prayer, reading and contemplation.

But in the middle of this life of prayer Mother Teresa and her nuns were working to change the world. They were working tirelessly to comfort the poor and dying. Mother Teresa said she did this because she saw the face of Christ in every poor person. She could only recognise the face of Christ in the poor because she had spent so long gazing on the face of Christ in contemplation. Mother Teresa and her nuns set an example for all Christians: prayer is the engine for changing the world.

Haves and have-nots

Mother Teresa's work is just one example of Christianity in action. There are thousands of examples of different ways that Christians work out their own salvation by ministering to others. Down through history more schools, hospitals, clinics, universities and feeding programmes have been started and staffed by Christians than by all other groups put together.

Driven by their life of prayer, and motivated by the example of Jesus Christ, Christians have been at the forefront of the battle against poverty and injustice in all its forms. It is true that there are wealthy and corrupt Christians. Every religion has hypocrites. But it is also true that Christians continually work with the poor to relieve the symptoms of poverty and to help them establish a better life.

Those who work with the poor are the front line soldiers. There are others who work from home administering charities, educating the public about the needs of the poor and working hard not just to treat the symptoms, but to address the root problems of poverty.

This Christian battle against poverty goes on in every country; in the cities and in the countryside. It goes on where famine and disaster strike and where ordinary conditions force people to live lives of misery and squalor.

If you want to change the world there are a multitude of ways for your Christian faith to help you get involved and make a difference. The only thing that is lacking is our own determination and hard work.

Peace and justice

If Christians are hard at work relieving poverty, they are also busy trying to establish peace and justice in the world. It is true that some Christian leaders actually lead the way in forcing through unjust laws. Some Christian leaders lead their country into war and are aggressive against weaker neighbours. Sometimes the church leaders have supported unjust regimes because they have been promised protection.

But for every hypocritical Christian who wages war, violates peace or causes injustice there are hundreds standing up for the rights of the oppressed, fighting for justice and working for peace in the world.

This too, is Christianity in action. Furthermore, the Christian who prays and worships is committed to working for peace and justice in his own life. He or she should constantly ask themselves if they are doing enough to live a simple life, to help the poor and to make sure they are not cheating in any way.

Think what the world would be like if everyone were honest. Think what the world would be like if everyone did their best, never made a quarrel worse and always sought for fairness and justice for all. What a wonderful world it could be!

We cannot make such a world overnight, but if every Christian person were to take their faith seriously and try even a little bit harder, then the world would be a better place for everyone.

Reconciliation and forgiveness

I cannot change the world, but with God's help I can change myself. I cannot take away all the suffering and pain in the world, but I can start with the pain and suffering that I cause other people.

If a Christian takes his faith seriously, then he or she must always be on the lookout for ways to make things better within their own life and within their own relationships.

The world is poisoned by jealousy, pride, envy, hatred, bitterness and the desire for revenge. It is a Christian's responsibility to address these problems in his own heart, in his own life and in his own relationships. Real change is possible, and the only thing that holds us back is our own attachment to bitterness, lust, hatred and love of revenge.

If we were to allow the Holy Spirit to rule our lives and direct us, then we would have the courage to reach out to those who have offended us with forgiveness. We would have the courage to build new relationships of love and justice. We would have the insight to be happy with what we have rather than seeking for more, more, more.

The Christian faith is practical. It works. All the religious activity is meant to get us to the point where Jesus Christ is so much a part of us that he works through us to bring about his will in the world. The battle against evil really can be won. Suffering really can be defeated. The world can be changed. And the change starts right where I am at this present moment in time.

Starting where we are

Mother Teresa started where she was. She was just another nun teaching in a school for girls. Once she got permission to start working amongst the poor she moved to a slum in Calcutta and did what she could do. She was a teacher. She started teaching the slum children. She didn't have any training as a nurse so she got some and started ministering to the health needs of the poor as well. Eventually some of her former students came to help her and the now famous order came into being.

Each one of us can begin to change ourselves and to change the world, and we can start where we are. Every journey begins with the first step. It might seem that you are a nobody. Wonderful. It is always people who know they are nobody who change the world for the best. It might seem that you have no gifts. The best gifts are not wealth, education and brilliance, but a heart and mind totally transformed by the power of the Holy Spirit.

Right now, this very day you can decide to change yourself and follow Christ into the amazing future he has prepared for you. Right now, this very day you can decide to work with him to change the world as much as you can. Right now, where you are, you can decide to make the most of your gifts and the most of who you are and spend the rest of your life making the world a better place. Right now, whoever you are, you can decide to fight the great fight against evil, or give in to that evil. Remember, if you are not contributing to the good you are allowing the evil to win.

Climb every mountain

No one promises that the fight will be easy. Indeed, deciding to fight against evil and live for Christ is the hardest thing you will ever decide to do. You will constantly stumble and fall in your effort to live a better life. That's okay. It doesn't matter how often you fall. It matters how often you get up.

If you decide to live the Christian life you will discover that the church is full of hypocrites. Other Christians will let you down. Christian leaders will turn out to be sinners and shallow, self-centred frauds. Your Christian friends will show themselves to be weak-willed, lazy and unwilling to help in the battle. Then, if you have any insight, you will realise that they are all just like you.

Don't imagine that the Christian life will be a nice, easy life full of wonderful spiritual experiences and happy religious time. You will get discouraged. There will be dark times. Remember, you are engaged in a war. You may think at times that you will never win. You may despair as you lose battle after battle. You may be tempted to give up, and at the end you will be convinced that the darkness is greater than the light.

In fact, like climbing a mountain, the further you go on this journey, the harder it will become. But also, like climbing a mountain, the further you go, the better the views are. The air is clearer and you have become stronger than you ever imagined you can be.

Are you up to the challenge? No one can do it alone. That is why I have said that we are accompanied and helped on the journey by all the others who have also decided to follow Christ. The final book in this series will help you explore the Christian Church in more detail and help you to understand more about the amazing army of God that has become your new family.

Additional Reading

The New Testament
The Catechism of the Catholic Church

Christian Classics
Mere Christianity by C.S. Lewis
The Screwtape Letters by C.S. Lewis
Orthodoxy by G.K. Chesterton
The Everlasting Man by G.K. Chesterton
The Creed in Slow Motion by Ronald Knox
Early Christian Writings by Maxwell Staniforth
The Penguin Dictionary of Saints by Donald Attwater
and Catherine Rachel Jones

Modern Catholic Books
Catholic Lives by Greg Watts - a collection of stories
of people who have become Catholic.

The Path to Rome by Dwight Longenecker - a more
weighty collection of conversion stories than
Catholic Lives.

More Christianity by Dwight Longenecker - this book
explains the Catholic faith in a friendly way to non-
Catholic Christians.

Adventures in Orthodoxy by Dwight Longenecker - a witty and colourful exploration of Christian belief.

Exploring the Catholic Church by Marcellino D'Ambrosio - a good small introduction to the Catholic Church today.

What Catholics Really Believe by Karl Keating - exploration of the Catholic faith in a question and answer format.

Knowing the Real Jesus by David Mills - a well written exploration of what the first Christians thought about Jesus Christ.

Surprised by Truth by Patrick Madrid - three volumes of American conversion stories.

Where is that in the Bible? and *Where is that in Tradition?* by Patrick Madrid - easy to read Catholic answers written in a punchy style.

What to do next...

You can order one or all of the other books in the CTS Christianity Pure & Simple series:

1. Is Anybody There? (Ref Do 699)

2. The God Man (Ref Do 700)

3. The Fire Of Life (Ref Do 701)

4. The Great Battle (Ref Do 702)

5. Welcome Home (Ref Do 703)

The quickest way to order is to call CTS direct on 020 7640 0042

You can send us a fax if you wish, on 020 7640 0046

Or pop your order in the post to:
CTS, 40-46 Harleyford Road,
Vauxhall, London SE11 5AY

Or visit our website
www.cts-online.org.uk/pureandsimple.htm

If this book has interested you and you want to discover more about Christianity then you may also find useful the following list of organisations:

www.faithcafe.org
If perhaps you already have some familiarity with the Catholic Church, but would like to explore some of the themes you've read about in this series, your local church may run Catholic Faith Exploration or CaFE

Catholic Enquiry Office
For enquiries about becoming a Catholic, knowing more about the Church or finding your local parish church. 114 West Heath Road, London NW3 7TX; Tel: 020 8458 3316; Email: ceo@cms.org.uk